FACING YOUR FEAR OF BUGS

BY RENEE BIERMANN

PEBBLE
a capstone imprint

Published by Pebble, an imprint of Capstone
1710 Roe Crest Drive, North Mankato, Minnesota 56003
capstonepub.com

Library of Congress Cataloging-in-Publication Data is available on the Library of Congress website.
ISBN: 9780756574154 (hardcover)
ISBN: 9780756574048 (paperback)
ISBN: 9780756574116 (ebook PDF)

Summary: Describes the reasons for fearing bugs and simple tips to overcome these fears.

Editorial Credits
Editor: Erika L. Shores; Designer: Heidi Thompson; Media Researcher: Jo Miller; Production Specialist: Tori Abraham

Image Credits
Getty Images: fstop123, Cover, Imgorthand, 13, Mint Images, 16, ronniechua, 6, Tim Hall, 19; Shutterstock: Domira (background), cover and throughout, Irina Kozorog, 7, Japan's Fireworks, 18 (firefly), Shutterstock: Juliya Shangarey, 10, Kapitosh (cloud), cover and throughout, konstantinos69, 20 (clothespin), Marian Fil, 15, Marish (brave girl), cover and throughout, Mega Pixel, 20 (glue), MERCURY studio, 9, Olga Popova, 20 (pipe cleaners), Olya Detry, 20 (pom-poms), Olya Humeniuk, 5, Paopano, 21 (googly eyes), Pepew Fegley, 18 (leaf bug), PictureDesignSwiss, 11, Tyler Fox, 17

All internet sites appearing in back matter were available and accurate when this book was sent to press.

Printed and bound in China.   PO5377

TABLE OF CONTENTS

Words in **bold** are in the glossary.

WHY BUGS CAN SCARE US

"Stop bugging me!" You have probably heard someone say that before. Bugs often bother people. Sometimes they fly near us and won't go away. Sometimes they give us itchy bites.

Bugs are all around us. More bugs live on Earth than we can count! You don't have to like bugs. But you can learn how to be less afraid of them.

Why are some people afraid of bugs? Some people are **allergic** to bugs. A bug bite or **sting** can make them sick. Other people get surprised by bugs. They are shocked when they see one!

Sometimes our fears come from other
people. We might know a friend who is
afraid of bugs. It can make us afraid too.

WHAT ARE BUGS FOR?

Learning about something we are afraid of can help us. The more we know, the less fear we will feel. Let's think about what bugs are for.

Bees and wasps visit flowers and plants. They move **pollen** from one place to another. This helps plants grow and make more plants.

9

It's surprising to walk into a spider's web! But spiders aren't trying to catch you. They're trying to catch other bugs! You can think of a spider as a teammate. It's keeping other bugs away.

Some bugs help us get food to eat. Ladybugs stop **pests** from hurting **crops**. Ground beetles move soil around. They eat other bugs and break down waste.

BUG SAFETY

Another way to fight fear is to know how to stay safe. Stay safe outside by asking an adult to help you put on bug spray. Always wear shoes to protect your feet. Wear long pants. Tuck your pants into your socks. Lastly, don't swat at bees or wasps. Stand still until they go away.

What happens if a bug bites or stings you? Tell an adult. Describe what the bug looked like. Try to not scratch the spot. Bug bites are annoying. But most bites won't hurt you. And the spot will go away quickly.

The truth is that most bugs don't want to bite people. They want to look for food. They want to build homes.

HOW TO ENJOY BUGS

You can be brave when you see a bug.
Stand near the bug. What do you see?

Try to learn three things about the bug. What color is it? How many legs does it have? Does it have **antenna**? Antenna are usually on a bug's head. What else do you notice about the bug?

You can see how interesting bugs can be. Watch some videos to learn more. Ask an adult to help you find videos about a bug that makes light. Look for videos of bugs that look like leaves.

You don't have to *love* bugs. They can still "bug" you. But you can be less afraid. You can be brave around bugs!

MAKE A BUG FRIEND

You can be friends with a bug.
Make one yourself! Play with your bug.
Take it outside to look at other bugs.
What can you learn together?

What You Need

- a wooden clothespin
- glue
- pom-poms
- pipe cleaners
- googly eyes

What You Do

1. Glue three pom-poms to the clothespin. They will be the bug's body.

2. Use pipe cleaners to make legs. You can make antenna too.

3. Glue on googly eyes. Your bug can have as many eyes as you want.

4. Give your bug a name. Introduce yourself.

5. Go play and have fun. See what you can learn about other bugs together!

GLOSSARY

allergic (uh-LUR-jik)—having a harmful reaction to something; reactions often include sneezing, swelling, and rashes

antenna (an-TEN-uh)—a pair of organs on a bug's head that help it feel, smell, and explore the world

crop (KROP)—a plant that a farm grows in large amounts, usually for food

pest (PEST)—an animal that is bothersome to people or plants

pollen (POL-uhn)—a dusty part of a plant that helps it reproduce, or make other plants

sting (STING)—a wound caused by a sharp stinger on a bee, wasp, or other bug

READ MORE

Boelts, Maribeth. *Kaia and the Bees*. Somerville, MA: Candlewick Press, 2020.

Brydon, Alli. *Bugs*. Washington, D.C.: National Geographic Kids, 2022.

Respicio, Mae. *Read All About Bugs*. North Mankato, MN: Capstone, 2023.

INTERNET SITES

Bug Activity Coloring Page
twistynoodle.com/bug-activity-coloring-page/

George's Busy Day: Bug Catcher
pbskids.org/curiousgeorge/busyday/bugs/

The Big Bug Memory Game
natgeokids.com/uk/play-and-win/games/bug-memory-game/

INDEX

ABOUT THE AUTHOR

Renee Biermann enjoys writing books for children. She lives on a farm in Iowa, where there are many bugs. When a bug surprises her in the house, she stops and takes a deep breath to calm down. Then she puts the bug outside!